— Praise for Jack

Over 100 ★★★★★ reviews on the most trusted book review sites

Author of Eight #1 Best Sellers — Over 10,000 Downloads

"With *Bukowski's Ghost,* Jackson Dean Chase invokes the spirit of the greatest poet of our time with the respect and admiration he deserves. This is an honest, intense, and remarkable collection by **a fresh and powerful new voice.**"
—*Terry Trueman, Printz Honor author of* Stuck in Neutral

"Jackson Dean Chase has found a place on my shelf, the **dark** corner, where I hide my **twisted little secrets.**"
—*Tome Tender*

"Mr. Chase is an equal opportunity entertainer with a **wry sense of humor.**"
—*Frank Fronash, author of Night of the Six-Gun Gorilla*

"[Chase] **knows his craft**..."
—*Nate Philbrick, author of* The Little One

"He **continues to amaze me** with his creativity and darkness."
—*Fang Freakin' Tastic Reviews*

"From poems that make you shiver to stories you wish did not end, Jackson will have you **turning pages** wanting to read more."
—*Kindle reviewer*

— Books by Jackson Dean Chase —

Poetry

Raw Underground Poetry series:
    #1 Bukowski's Ghost
    #2 Love at the Bottom of the Litter Box

Fiction

Beyond the Dome series:
    #0 Hard Times in Dronetown
    #1 Drone
    #2 Warrior (coming soon)

Young Adult Horror series:
    #1 Come to the Cemetery
    #2 The Werewolf Wants Me
    #3 The Haunting of Hex House
    #4 Gore Girls: Twisted Tales & Poems
    #5 Lost Girls: Twisted Tales & Poems
    #6 Horror Girls: Twisted Tales & Poems
    #7 Killer Young Adult Fiction (complete series + extras)

Non-Fiction

How to Write Realistic Fiction series:
    #1 How to Write Realistic Characters
    #2 How to Write Realistic Men

Writers's Phrase Book series:
    #1 Horror Writers' Phrase Book
    #2 Post-Apocalypse Writers' Phrase Book
    #3 Action Writers' Phrase Book

— RAW UNDERGROUND POETRY —

Bukowski's GHOST

(Poems for Old Souls in New Bodies)

JACKSON DEAN CHASE

www.JacksonDeanChase.com

For Charles Bukowski, who taught me to love poetry,
and to his Ghost, for whispering in my ear.

Thanks to my editor, C. Graves, for years of heartfelt perseverance shaping my talent. This book would not exist without you, and I'm profoundly grateful.

Special thanks to my incredible Launch Team: Jen Crews, Melanie Marsh, Sherry Rentschler, Tina Simon, and Julie Stafford.

First Printing, November 2015

ISBN-13: 978-1519546067

ISBN-10: 1519546068

Published by Jackson Dean Chase, Inc.

Printed by CreateSpace

BUKOWSKI'S GHOST: Poems for Old Souls in New Bodies

Copyright © 2015 Jackson Dean Chase, Inc. All rights reserved.

Cover image used under license from jumpingsack / Shutterstock.com

Author photo by C. Graves. © 2015 Jackson Dean Chase, Inc.

Without limiting the rights under copyright above, no part of this book may be reproduced, stored in or introduced into a retrieval system or transmitted, in any form or by any means (electronic, mechanical, photocopying, recording, or otherwise), without the written consent of both the copyright holder and the above publisher of this book.

PUBLISHER'S NOTE

"Bold Visions of Dark Places" is a trademark of Jackson Dean Chase, Inc.

This is a work of fiction. Names, characters, places, and incidents are products of the author's imagination or are used fictitiously. Any resemblance to actual events or locales or persons, living or dead, is entirely coincidental.

The scanning, uploading, and distribution of this book via the Internet or via any other means without the written permission of the publisher is illegal and punishable by law. Please purchase only authorized electronic editions, and do not participate in or encourage electronic piracy of copyrighted materials. Your support of the author is appreciated.

For **FREE BOOKS** and More, Visit the Author at:

www.JacksonDeanChase.com

CONTENTS

9	Welcome, Friend! (an original epigraph)
11	Introduction

— *Part One: THE HEART OF THE POET*
(Meditations on the Creative Struggle)

15	The Last Man on Earth
17	The Darkest Thoughts
18	Silence Is Deadly
19	Million Moron March
20	When the Words Die
21	The Fuckery of the Mob
22	The Art of Being Evil
24	This War
25	Weep Now, My Lovely
26	Replaced
27	What Life Is
29	Paralyzed
30	This Motherfucking Life
31	More Than Normal
32	The Poetry Devil
33	One Last Poem
34	True Poems
35	This Cold, Dead World
36	Taste the Pain
38	My First Three Months
39	I'm Better at Pain
40	The Life of a Hermit
43	The Man I Could Have Been
45	A Letter to the Old Me
46	I Am the Catalyst
48	The Incredible Melting Men
49	I Am God Now

50	These Hands
51	When the Pain Gets Too Much
52	The Only Way
53	The Woman Thing
56	Upfront
57	Too Many Poems
58	Where Do You Get Your Inspiration?
59	The Lost Poet
60	I've Still Got Time
62	Inner Child
63	The Next Great Challenge
64	The First Day
65	The Heart of the Poet

— Part Two: ANOTHER WASTED NIGHT
(Meditations on Anger, Loneliness, and Despair)

69	Another Wasted Night
70	Hot Dogs for the Hopeless
71	My Heart is a Convenience Store
72	Death March to the Food Bank
73	The Last Roll
74	Lost
75	Skinny Tiger and Fatty Dragon
77	Small Town Secrets
78	From Jekyll to Hyde in 12-Fluid Ounces
79	A Nose for Trouble
80	Despair
81	One-Night Stand
82	Pure Love
83	My Life is Slow Death
84	Better This Way
85	Five Words
86	Abandoned, Betrayed
87	Waiting to Die

88	Riders on the Bus
90	Gray
91	Alphabet of Suffering
92	Family
93	Hell is My Home Address
94	Another Holiday in Hell
95	The Happiest Time of the Year
96	Government Cheesecake
97	Broken Dreams
98	Garbage People
99	A Warning to Girls
100	America
101	It's All the Same
102	Drifting
103	Right and Wrong
104	It's Killing Us
105	Circling the Drain
106	Weakness
107	Self-Deception
108	The Gondola of My Fears
109	Civil War
110	Regret

— Part Three: THE GHOST IN ME
(Meditations on Life, Death, and Beyond)

113	The Long, Slow Monday
114	These Shoes, They Travel
115	The Bitter Days of Autumn
116	Without Hope
117	The Worst Way to Die
118	Worthless
119	The Mystery Tree
122	End of the Line
123	Might As Well Enjoy It

124	Suicide Solution
125	Suicide Note
126	Meat Suit
127	A Meditation on Death
128	This Dusty Soul
129	Nursing Home Blues
130	Time is a Bastard
131	Done
132	The Disappointed Life
133	This Amnesiac World
134	Like Flowers
135	The Show Must Go On
136	When No One Cares
137	The Struggle
138	The Problem with Words
139	Blind
140	Something for Nothing
141	And Soon, the Snow
142	Everyday, There Are People
143	If You Want My Advice
144	The Strangest Places
145	The Road Within
146	Nobody's Perfect
148	At Peace, At Last
149	No Looking Back
150	Ready for the Rain
151	You Know You're Getting Old
152	Old Souls
153	Always a Challenge
154	Bukowski's Ghost
155	The Ghost in Me

— *Bonus: MY POETRY MANIFESTO*

156	Advice to New Poets

WELCOME, FRIEND!

Life is a mad story
told one day
at a time.

– Warning –

Although I am perhaps best known as a prolific writer of Young Adult fiction, the poems in this book are intended for mature audiences.

— Introduction —

People love me. People hate me. And I do a little of both. What you are about to read is my personal poetry. Words I bled for, words I own as much as they own me. With them, you can see not just into the deepest part of my soul, but into your own darkness, your own light. You might be surprised what you find.

Life is pain, life is love. It's also short, and I'm tired of wasting mine hiding from the world. I want to share myself. I want to be with you now, in this moment.

And so I am.

I came to poetry late in life. I'd never thought much of it. Shakespeare and all that fancy shit did nothing for me. Then I discovered Charles Bukowski, the greatest poet of the twentieth century, and the first to truly give poetry back to the people. He did that by writing in plain English about what was real, and what the common man could connect with. Reading him lit that same fire in me. No doubt he lit a similar one in you.

It is Bukowski's ghost that inspires us: me to write these words, and you to read them. Live them, feel them. Forever.

Your Fellow Misfit,
Jackson Dean Chase
www.JacksonDeanChase.com

— *Part One* —
THE HEART OF THE POET
(Meditations on the Creative Struggle)

The Last Man on Earth

The landscape's in ruins
and all the dogs have run away,
but you're still here:
    the last man on earth.
Stupid and alone,
the way you've always been.
And everyone is dead,
the way you've always wanted.
The world's real peaceful.
You have time now:
    no bills to pay,
    no work to do.
Except staying alive has become a chore.
You do it anyway,
convinced there is some value in going on.
After all, there are still poems to write—
    the ones you promised wouldn't suck.
And so you write them in blood
on city walls and broken streets.
You write them in your own filth
and wear your fingers down to stumps,
until they are no more than bones
scratching in the dirt.

And when the last poem has been written,
you read them to the wind,

to the bombed-out factories,
to the buzzards circling overhead.
You read them to God,
and when you get sick of Him,
you read to other gods:
    to Zeus and Odin, Buddha, Vishnu.
You even read to the Devil and all his demons.
You read them to the ghosts of those you knew,
and those you thought you knew.
You read them to your idols,
to old Bukowski and Artaud,
spinning in their graves.
But no one answers.
They've all moved on
to other bodies, other worlds.

    Why stop at ruining this one?

The Darkest Thoughts

Sometimes, the darkest thoughts
hide in the light where they can be accepted—
embraced for what they pretend,
    not what they are.
Look around and you'll find them.
Our world is built on darkness disguised as:
    government,
    society,
    business,
    religion.
They call my darkness sick, twisted.
    And maybe it is,
        but at least it's honest.

SILENCE IS DEADLY

Silence is as deadly an enemy to the torturer
as it is to the poet:

> *We both want to hear*
> *   our audience scream.*

Million Moron March

No villain can compare to
the dull horror of an empty mind.
For when you bring enough of them together,
you get an unruly Mob, a nation of fools.
Slack-jawed in its ignorance,
loudly proclaiming it knows best,
when it knows nothing but
    how to eat,
    how to sleep,
    how to fuck.
The Mob does not understand anything of value
because it offers nothing of value.
It delights in garbage because it is garbage,
feeding on it, rolling in it like pigs.
Even now, the Mob marches to destroy
    all that we know,
    all that we are.
It seeks nothing more than total victory
over everyone who is not Average,
who does not, or cannot conform.
The Mob seeks to kill
    the intellectuals,
    the poets,
    the dreamers.
The Mob will not stop until we are dead,
our voiceless husks trampled in the streets.

When the Words Die

When the words die, people die.
    Not in body,
    but in spirit.
They shuffle around like zombies,
Feeding animal needs for animal brains.
They're sick with it,
    sick with knowing
    and not knowing.
Wanting more,
    but accepting less.
They burned all the books
to keep the fire of ignorance alive.
Independent thought crushed,
independent voices silenced.
Only the fools speak now
with guns and bombs.
These are the new words,
the only language that is spoken:
    one common tongue,
    one hateful sound
    echoing into infinity.

The Fuckery of the Mob

The fuckery of the mob is a powerful thing,
but left to its own devices,
it will always do the wrong thing,
    the easy thing.
To be a scalpel instead of a sword,
the mob must be ruled
by sinister men with sinister minds
    in boardrooms,
    in churches,
    in government offices,
    and underground bunkers.
Only then can the mob
be used to create instead of destroy.

The Art of Being Evil

Pain, the paintbrush of the sadist.
Insults, the poems of the ignorant.
Oppression, the music of the jealous.
Evil creates art according to its own needs,
expressing it as:
    torture,
    humiliation,
    the police state,
    and finally, religion.
From schoolyard taunts to nuclear war,
the world is its canvas, our screams, its words.
It finds its melody in:
    the marching of booted feet,
    the angry cheer of empty minds,
    in bullets, in bombs,
    slavery and despair.
Evil strives for immortality yet always fails,
thinking itself invincible
when it is even more fragile than good.
Eventually, it must be unmasked,
    overthrown,
its devils revealed not as gods,
but as small men with sick minds.
Greedy, gloating parasites.
Unloved,
    venomous, cancerous.

Human tumors that must be cut out!
One by one, they fall,
betraying each other as they betrayed us.
We drive them out and forget
    until the next masterpiece is born.

THIS WAR

There is a war in this country—
    a war on me, and people like me:
Artists, writers, musicians, poets,
    anyone who dreams too long or too deeply.
Anyone who looks within,
instead of at the bread and circuses the media serves us.
This feast of shit assaults our senses
through every channel, every day.
This war will go on, ceaseless,
    churning out corpses with crushed souls,
        shattered men with broken hearts
            and the women who weep for them.
This war is on independent thinkers, on those who stand
    outside the law,
        outside the rules,
            outside sick societal norms.
They persecute us
because they cannot kill us any other way.
Their feeble vanity prevents the gun to the face.
They find public execution distasteful
and prefer private ones:
    the long death,
        the slow death,
            inches at a time.
The death meted out in bars and back alleys,
    vomiting hope into the gutter.

They prefer the noose of obligation,
   the electric chair of anger,
      and slipping arsenic in your morning coffee—
         just enough to keep you from dying.
They want you weak.
   They want you stupid.
      They want you drunk and drugged,
         too stoned to go on.
They want you in the madhouse or in prison
   so they can take away your pen,
      your paint,
         your guitar,
            your computer,
               whatever tools you need to create.
They will deny them to you
saying it's for your own good,
that they could be used as weapons . . .
because they can.

And in the end, once they have
   taken all these things,
      then they will come for your soul.

Weep Now, My Lovely

Weep now, my lovely.
Weep for this world that does not care,
these tyrants who will not die,
who go on suffering
and cause suffering in return.
Weep for those they kill,
those they rob of innocence,
    of youth,
    of joy,
but most of all, of freedom.

Weep for me as I sit alone
in a crowded room,
typing these words,
wishing they weren't true.
I long for a better life,
a better world,
knowing I will die as I have lived:
    Unloved.

Weep now, my lovely.
Weep for yourself
reading this poem,
living these words.

Replaced

The world changes
too fast to keep up.
Just when you think
you understand it,
they pull the rug out:
    technology,
    music,
    fashion,
    morality.
All dead, replaced by newer models—
    as you have been, as we all must be
    until the bombs drop,
    the plague hits,
    and the last light goes out
    forever.

What Life Is

I don't know why I want to be a poet.
It just seems terribly important now,
despite hating poems my whole life.
The only poet I really love
is Charles Bukowski.
That sad old man,
the vulgar man with the alcoholic soul.
He's the one who makes the words look easy
because sometimes he's not very good.
He talks too much about racetracks and whores
and all the shitty people in his life,
but most of all, he talks about the booze.
I don't gamble or chase whores
I don't drink (well, not too much),
and I don't let shitty people into my life—
at least not after that last bunch.
In fact, I hardly let anyone in at all
except my two cats,
and sometimes, even they feel like too much,
but they're better than having no one at all.
I spend all day hunched over my computer
wanting to write half as good as Bukowski.
Bukowski at his best,
when he wasn't drunk or not drunk enough
to write about his boring day
instead of his interesting life.

I write until my brain hurts and my fingers bleed,
a red smear of truth from the bucket of my soul.
Now it's late, past midnight.
I have to piss.
I go to the bathroom,
    trip over the cats,
    hit the light,
    and whip out my dick.
I pick up that new book of Bukowski poems,
one of five hundred released after he died.
I open to a random page,
hoping for a chuckle
or some kind of inspiration,
but it's another boring one about booze.
The worst part is
I think my dick's aiming into the toilet,
but it's really pointed at the floor.

PARALYZED

Another empty day gone by.
The sun & moon have met in some dark corner and fucked,
giving birth to this dread,
this haunting whisper that says,
    "You let the time slip away again. You should have been writing, reading, working . . . Instead, you sat here and did nothing."
The voice says you'll never be rich or famous,
never be anything at all:
    Just some loser sitting in a shabby studio apartment
        with the TV too loud,
            the rent past due,
                and no one to hear
                      your soul screaming for help.

THIS MOTHERFUCKING LIFE

Have you ever felt dejected, rejected,
    cast down and out?
Well, I have, baby.
Every fucking day of
    this motherfucking life!
Of course, some days are better than others:
    the days when I write,
    and the nights when I dream
    of something other than pain.
But these are small triumphs
    in an otherwise empty world . . .
A world where I can't trust anyone
    not to hate me.
        (Secretly, or to my face).
Where every hand that feeds me
    suddenly bites back, fingers digging in,
    clawing, crushing everything I am
    and trying to inject everything I'm not.
Even if I wanted to change,
    I can't.

More Than Normal

To try to be anything more than normal
    is to be told you are less.
It is the cruelest torture, the sweetest poison:
    the fast mocking of others,
    the slow hating of self.
An endless struggle of back-and-forth lies.
And for what?
A brief moment of happiness?
That too is a lie!
Happiness fades,
joy cannot be sustained
leaving you worse for having tasted its kiss.
Better to give up, give in.
Wait it out, like so many before you:
    Nameless,
    Forgotten,
    Normal.
Abandon your dreams now:
    Surrender!
Become one of the crowd, the bleating sheep:
    Ignorant, oblivious,
        uncaring on your way to slaughter.
It will only hurt for a minute
then you won't feel anything at all . . .

The Poetry Devil

The Poetry Devil is back,
banging at my mind.
He's never gone long,
just long enough
    to sharpen his teeth,
    his horns,
    his tail,
and yes, the tiny pitchfork
that pokes and prods,
puncturing my brain.
    Letting his ideas in,
    and my words out . . .
They are one and the same.

True Poems

True poems are not safe:
    They must murder some part of you
        while giving birth to another . . .

This Cold, Dead World

I don't want to work anymore.
Not for them,
and not for you,
but only for me.
Mad, irrepressible me:
    the writer,
        the poet,
            the dreamer.
I want to spend every minute
I have inside my head
instead of out here in
this cold, dead world.

Taste the Pain

To know this dream,
to live this poet's life,
you must first taste pain.
Rolling it in your mouth
like fine wine,
tasting all the subtle notes of
    shame,
    rage,
    sorrow.
The flavors are memories
taking you back
to the worst pain
you've ever known:

  See it,
    touch it,
      taste it!

Let it fill you with
    smoke.
Let it fill you with
    ashes.
Let it fill you with
    regret, with longing.
Let it destroy you,
burning you to nothing.

Only then can you be free
to express your pain—
 the whole of it,
 the truth of it.
Not just in words,
 but feelings.

My First Three Months

In three months, I have written over 500 poems
    and completed my second novel,
in addition to maintaining a daily blog
    and social media presence.
I have editors at four publishers
    wanting to see my new book.
Instead of being proud of this,
    I berate myself for not doing more.
I point out I wrote 164 poems the first month
    and 235 the second.
This third month, I only wrote 95.
    Ninety-fucking-five!
    That hurts.
I see it as proof I'm slipping.
What's wrong with me?
Why am I so lazy?
Never mind the novel took up most of my time,
    it's the poetry that matters.
After all, what kind of goddamn poet can't write
    a hundred poems a month?

I'm Better at Pain

I write poems.
They're easier than everything else,
    faster too.
I write at least one poem a day:
    The average is five,
    but my record's fifteen.
Not fifteen good ones, mind you—
    just fifteen.
Most of them
    (the best ones)
    are about pain.
The rest are about hope
    or faith,
    even love.
I mean them just as much,
    if not more,
    but I'm better at pain.
I spent most of my life with it.
    I know it.
Pain clings to me like a lover,
    the one I can't let go.

The Life of a Hermit

On any given day, I will
    wake up,
    curse,
    crack my knuckles,
    stare at the ceiling,
    wish for another hour of sleep,
    wish for a whole new life,
    rise and pet the cats,
        tell them they are beautiful,
    then piss,
    and pour myself an energy drink.

I will stare at my computer
    expecting today is the day
    I will be discovered
    and everything will change.

I will answer emails,
    tweet and retweet things,
    check my blog stats,
    eat a processed meat stick,
    open a document,
    and write.

When the time comes, I will take a shit,
    reading Bukowski on the toilet,

    taking comfort in his words.

I will eat a sandwich and watch TV,
    wanting my life to be like a sitcom
    instead of a tragedy.

I will write some more poems,
    take another shit
    like a hobbit's second breakfast.
    While I am there,
    I will jot down a few poems by hand
    as I wait for it all to come out
    (the words and the shit).

Then I go back to the computer,
    check my email, my social media.
I'm still not famous, so I curse
    and break things
        until the cats look at me in alarm.

I eat dinner and watch TV, maybe a movie—
    an old one, like my soul.
After the movie is over, I take a shower.
    I'll even get dressed,
    though I have nowhere to go.

I stare at myself in the mirror:
    getting older, poorer,
    more desperate,

more loved yet unloved,
more real yet less real.

I clean the cats' litter box
    and can't believe how two tiny animals
    can fill three boxes so consistently.
I sigh, remembering the cats are my only friends
    so I will accept their shit, as they accept mine.

I stare into the night,
at the train tracks and the train on it.
I want to run out of my apartment
    and ride the rails like a hobo.
I want the train to take me far from here,
    far from this miserable life,
but I am tired and it is too late to run—
    from here or anywhere.

I go to sleep and dream,
    hoping tomorrow will be different,
        but secretly,
            I know
                it will be
                    just
                        the
                            same.

The Man I Could Have Been

I sit in my cabin as I write this,
rain and wind my only companions.
The small, crackling fire of my existence
cooling now to embers.
I listen to the storm
and drink from the bottle—
    the last of the good stuff,
    and like this poem,
    the last of me.
This life has been a hard one.
I had no map, no guides,
no friends or family.
I had no one but myself
and some vague idea
which way to go.
Fortune, fame, love, respect,
all these things eluded me,
    deluded me
into thinking I deserved them,
that I'd know what to do
when the time came . . .

All my dreams of gold became bitter brass.
Poor, tarnished torments,
the haunting whispers of "What if?"
echo in my mind.

This road was longer than I thought,
made of dusty, uneven ground.
Ground that shook,
shifting with hidden danger
just when I thought I had arrived at last.
The mountain I had meant to climb buries me
    alone, forgotten.

And the wind does blow, the skies do weep.
Not for the man I was,
    but the man I could have been.

A Letter to the Old Me

I am the Invincible Man,
the Impossible Man,
born to do Great Things:
    to be more than you
        because I am willing to dare more,
    to risk my very soul.
I will rise up, and in my rising,
    I will crush you,
        destroying the terrible past
        to make way for the glorious future.
You had your chance and you blew it
    you fool, you dumb fuck!
Now, I am here,
    here to stay,
    to be everything you could not
    while you are Nothing,
    becoming less than Nothing
    until you are finally
    forgotten.

I Am the Catalyst

Why does everyone say I take
when all I do is give?
I take ordinary, useless lives
and transform them,
giving them a chance to know greatness:
    theirs and mine.
It is not enough.
They all reject me,
fail to understand I am the Catalyst,
    the Bringer of Change.
They are too blind, too scared to see,
and so they find ways to attack
    my beliefs,
    my self-esteem,
    my confidence,
    my appearance,
    my clothes,
    my taste,
    and finally, my art.
The great works I have bled for,
they dare to dismiss
and would destroy me if I let them.
Everyone has the potential for greatness,
but few know it,
and even fewer are willing
to embrace this path

because they know the frightened Mob
will only try to pull them down:
    friends, family, lovers,
      even your fellow artists.
It's all the same.
They will show anger
when they should show appreciation.
They will shed tears of self-pity
when they should know happiness.
They will slam the brakes on success
just when they should hit the gas.
That is their tragedy,
but it doesn't have to be yours.

    Cut them out,
      chop them down.
        Erase them and move on!

What can people give you art can't?
The answer, my friend, is pain.

The Incredible Melting Men

All these plastic people with plastic minds
melt in the heat of my dreams:
not understanding, not believing
in anything that does not
come out of a box or a can.
They think they know how to live,
but they only know how to die!
    They die the slow way,
    the hard way,
    pressing buttons,
    pushing gears.
They are melting more each day,
forming sticky puddles of rotted flesh
on carpets,
on sidewalks,
and in the street.
These fools melt,
spreading their sickness,
yet dare judge me
because my choice is to be
wild beneath sun-bright skies,
rising up instead of
melting down.

I Am God Now

I am God now.
My blood is ink,
and I sacrifice you,
    my Words,
my only begotten Sons,
on the cross of my dreams.
Waiting for you to rise,
    to BE
what I could not.

These Hands

Some nights, I stare at these hands
and can't believe what they've done—
a hundred lives lived, a million more lost.
These hands are not done,
they must continue
    creating,
       destroying,
until time does what the blank page could not:
       defeat me.

When the Pain Gets Too Much

When the pain gets too much,
    when you are sick of being everything
    you never wanted to be,
    that is the perfect time to reinvent yourself.
Put your mind to it!
Fill your heart with song,
    your mind with verse.
Let the power of intention fill you,
    let it guide you like a missile
    to your true purpose,
    your one desire.
Imagine it . . .
    Now become it.

THE ONLY WAY

Happy is the man who knows not, is not, does not.
For to know,
    to be,
    to do,
is the Hard Way, the Way of Pain.
It is every hell that is or will ever be.
It is unyielding, impossible,
and yet, for some,
it is the Only Way.

    Walk it with me.

The Woman Thing

Things have been bothering me lately—
not a lot, but enough.
There's always the money thing,
the career thing,
but worst of all is the woman thing.
That's what's eating me now:
    The memory of you.
In my house, I can't forget.
So I put on my black leather jacket
and pull my baseball cap low,
stepping into cold November rain.
I take a long walk to clear my head.
I don't look at the people smoking on doorsteps
    or hurrying past.
This isn't about meeting anyone
    (that's the last thing I need).
I just want to be alone with myself:
    no bills,
    no internet,
    no women,
just me and the night.

It's quiet out, peaceful.
The rain isn't bad, and I even manage to whistle a tune.
Not too cheerful, but it's a start.
I walk to the library,

drawing inspiration from the shelves.
I check out some books by Bukowski,
and a DVD of his poetry readings.

When I get home, I feel better.
The cats greet me at the door,
an onslaught of head-bonks to show their love.
I check my messages, relieved you haven't called
    (no one has).
I pop Buk's DVD into the computer.
The crazy old man appears on the screen,
drunk and rowdy as ever.
The audience loves Buk as much he hates them,
and maybe that's a metaphor for our relationship:
    Love, hate.
      Hate, love.
    Both of us sick with separate needs—
      you, desperately trying to get in,
        me, desperately trying to get out.
But I want to forget all that, so I return to the show.
It's a beautiful riot, the old man vs. the mob.
    They're evenly matched
    as the wine flows
    and the words come.

Point the way, Buk.
Point the way!

Halfway through, he does.

Inspiration hits, or maybe it's the wine.
I write a poem, a damn good one—
    one I can hear Buk narrating in my mind.
And when it's done, I write another,
and another . . .

The best time to write is when
the pain's still fresh,
the hurt's too deep.

It makes me glad the women leave
because I get to keep these poems instead.

Upfront

When I was a child, I took the bus to school.
Dull orange, it reeked of
    conformity and stale promises,
    decades of lies pledged to the allegiance
    of unmarked graves.
I always sat behind the driver
so I could be alone with my thoughts,
far removed from the tyranny of others:
    those scabby little monsters
    who haunted the back rows
    preying on any kid who got too close.
Upfront, I was safe.
Upfront, I belonged to my own world,
my own kingdom.
It was a bright and shining place
where, for just a few minutes,
I could be free . . .

Too Many Poems

Sometimes, when I think
I've written too many poems
for them to be any good,
I think of Bukowski:
How he used to write ten a day,
maybe more.
Then I don't feel so bad.
Still, I wonder what Buk would think.
Would he hate my poems? Call me a hack?
Or encourage me to write more?
I'll never know.
Buk is dead, his genius gone,
though his ghost releases a new book every year.
Meanwhile, I'm alive, writing my first,
wondering if anyone will buy it,
will love me the way they loved him.
I swear, if they do,
I'll be just as flabbergasted as Buk,
but a hell of a lot more grateful.

Where Do You Get Your Inspiration?

Since I don't read much poetry,
I get most of my inspiration from song lyrics—
the darker, the better.
I'm talking bands like:
    The Sisters of Mercy,
    Nick Cave,
    Dio,
    The Doors . . .
Lyrics are another form of poetry,
the most popular form,
and the only kind most people will listen to
so it makes sense to learn from them.

They will be remembered and loved
far longer than any poet.
The masses will see to that.
They always do.

The Lost Poet

I write a lot of poems about Charles Bukowski,
but this one's about Antonin Artaud:
    French guy, quite mad.
He invented the "Theater of Cruelty"
and had a hard time finishing anything:
    Plays, stories, poems,
        all fell victim to his insane whims.
But he did all right
    (in-between the asylums and bad reviews).
Some called him a prophet, others a fool—
    a maniac lost to his own dreams.
But I'd rather be lost to my worst dreams
than your best reality.

I've Still Got Time

It was winter in the park: cold,
bitter with snow, with longing.
An old man sat on a bench
dreaming of better days,
of plump girls with pure hearts,
unfinished poems,
and unfulfilled promises.
Puffs of steam came from his mouth,
tears crystallized on his cheeks.
There was nothing more to do
except get another drink.
As the man stood,
there was pain in his chest, and in his knees.
Bad pain:
    buckling,
    crippling,
    almost causing him to fall.
But he caught himself,
    hands braced on the bench,
    hands braced against the years,
    against growing numb,
    against God and all his angels
    come to carry him home.
He would end his life as it had begun:
    with nothing,
    as nothing.

But the man did not want that.
He would not bend,
he would not die—not yet.
Gradually, the pain eased.
He let out a slow whoosh,
his breath tinged with hope.
The man had a sudden revelation of his true self,
his true purpose.
Now he was determined to finish his poems
and keep what promises he could.
"I've still got time," he thought as he hurried to his car.

Do you?

Inner Child

I'm happy to report my inner child is alive and well,
yet I see the graves of others all around me.
Don't let yours be one of them!
Stay young in the only way you can.
For me, it is writing.
For you, I cannot say,
but I know you can.
   Think!
What is the one thing that makes you happy?
What brings you the most joy,
the best feeling of success?
When you can answer without fear,
without doubt, or shame, or guilt,
when you know in your heart
there can be nothing else,
then you must do this one thing,
this great thing!

Do it! Do it now.
Your inner child is waiting.

The Next Great Challenge

To bend, but not break
is the goal society sets.
But all too often,
you bend the knee,
compromise the spirit
to spare the pain.
Sometimes, it is better
    to break,
tearing down what was
    for what must be.
Only when self-destruction
becomes self-creation
can it be controlled.
Only then can you gain
victory through defeat
and from your ashes, arise anew:
    remade, rebuilt, reborn,
    and ready to fight
    the next great challenge.

THE FIRST DAY

They say, "Today is the first day of the rest of your life."
So what are you still doing here reading this?
Why aren't you running around
    laughing
    fucking
    drinking
finding yourself in the company of others?
Maybe it's because you want to be alone,
to feel something only I can give you—
the kind of release that's less showy,
more secret.
The slow burn, that *"a-ha!"* moment
where something shakes loose and you feel
your true self, your true power!
The real you, carefree and beautiful.
The brilliant you, the doer of things.
Sublime creator of the impossible:
    the God-You,
    the Soul-You.
That innocent spirit that yearns
To express itself.
    DO IT!
Put down this poem and
    BE YOURSELF.
The one you were meant to be
from the first moment you came into this life.

The Heart of the Poet

The heart of the poet beats
for all those whose hearts have stopped,
whose minds have dulled,
who don't know how to live
or how to feel.

The heart of the poet beats
for the dreamers,
for the brave and unbroken,
for the young at heart
and old of soul.

The heart of the poet beats
for you, for me,
and this beautiful world
that bleeds at our touch.

— *Part Two* —
ANOTHER WASTED NIGHT
(Meditations on Anger, Loneliness, and Despair)

Another Wasted Night

I am drunk on regret, on knowing
I'll never be good enough.
This diner is old, comforting,
like my mother's hands.
I slide into a booth and order fries
wanting to taste love,
wanting to taste anything
but what I feel right now.

Hot Dogs for the Hopeless

Everyday, I come inside your air-conditioned bliss.
I buy a hot dog and a Coke just to see you.
I touch your hand on purpose
when I give you the money.
You are my only human connection,
    my most treasured moment,
    but you don't care.
I'm nobody in this nothing world:
    Nobody to you,
    Nobody to me.
The dinosaurs went extinct.
I wonder if I will,
waiting for you to notice me?

My Heart is a Convenience Store

My heart is a convenience store.
It's open 24/7 with a sign in the window
that begs, "Come in and save!"
In my youth, it wasn't so bad.
But like anything that stays open too long,
it begins to age
    with cracks in the walls
    and dust on the shelves.
Someday, my heart will close
    and never reopen.

Death March to the Food Bank

I wake up at half-past four feeling like shit,
all the aches of the world in my bones.
It's the end of the month,
nothing to eat.
I need to drag my ass to the food bank.
I pop my pills and pull on clothes,
enough to pass for human.
Outside, the rain comes down.
I stand on the corner, no umbrella, waiting.
The bus is ten minutes late.
I get on, flash my disabled pass, and take a seat.
I hate this trip!
It's not just humiliating,
it's a ride straight to hell.
What losers and crazies
will I have to put up with this time?
What indignities from the staff?
Madness! Destruction!
I stare out the window,
hating to numb the pain:
    myself, the world,
      it doesn't matter.
We're all to blame.

THE LAST ROLL

Is it selfish to hide
the last roll of toilet paper?
My roommate uses it
faster than I can buy it.
What should have lasted a month
is almost gone.
    Gone, like my patience.
    Gone, like my life.
I don't like being petty,
but I guess I can be.

Lost

I have lost many friends
    to the bottle,
    to needles and pills,
    to accidents and suicide.
I have lost them
    to New Age,
    to Old Age,
    to women and children,
    to abusive relationships,
    to greedy natures
    and suspicious minds.
I have lost them to me,
    to my faults,
    my burning ambition,
    indifference and need.
These were people I loved,
and who I thought loved me.

    But love is not enough
        in this world of lies.

Skinny Tiger
and Fatty Dragon

I knew this dumb fat kid growing up.
He was as round as he was evil
with eyes like jelly doughnuts
glazed with hate.
His dad owned a hamburger stand
and was even fatter than his son
    (but of course, he was much older
    and had eaten more hamburgers).
At any rate, this fat kid was my enemy.
I was smart and thin,
fair-haired, blue-eyed,
a golden boy destined for greatness.

One day, we decided to fight:
    Skinny Tiger and Fatty Dragon.
We got off the school bus
and I went into my combat stance.
Fatty just stood there,
an immovable lump
hating me through his dumb doughnut eyes.
I'd been practicing karate all summer,
watching Bruce Lee
and every ninja movie ever made.
I was really looking forward
to kicking his ass.

I gave him a roundhouse to the stomach,
but my foot just sank into his fat
like human quicksand.
It went in so deep, it touched his spine
    then bounced out,
    knocking me to the dirt.
Fatty just stood there, stupid and evil,
while the crowd laughed at me.
That fight is the story of my life.

Years pass, decades gone.
Fatty's father died,
but his hamburger stand is still there.
I drive by it sometimes,
    wondering how my enemy lives
        while I die a little more each day.

Small Town Secrets

The city has a million secrets,
the small town just a few.
But they are always worse
because you know these people,
or at least thought you did.
You feel stupid for not knowing,
not even guessing
how sick your neighbors really are.
And if they could have hidden *that*
all these years,
what else don't you know—
    not just about them,
      but yourself?

From Jekyll to Hyde in 12-Fluid Ounces

You don't need a magic potion
to turn a man into a monster.
Give him a few beers,
then stand back
and watch the fun.

A Nose for Trouble

The man was in his forties,
quite successful by the standards of others,
but he wasn't happy inside.
One day, a boil appeared on the end of his nose.
It bothered him a great deal,
so he pinched and he prodded,
but the boil refused to go.
Day after day went by,
    the boil growing larger
    as the man's self-esteem withered
    and it seemed he was more boil than man.
He'd almost given up, gotten used to
the revulsion of others and his own self-loathing.
Then one day, almost without provocation the boil burst,
squirting blood and stinking pus all over the mirror,
dripping onto his white shirt and power tie.
But the man was so relieved, he didn't care.
"I got you, you bastard!" he cried.
But he hadn't—the boil had got him instead.
The man's soul leaked through the hole,
and he felt sad for a moment,
then went back to doing his paperwork:
    Another soulless bureaucrat,
    a beaten machine.

Despair

I should have stayed,
I should have gone.
Instead, I find myself trapped
here, with you.

   Alone.

ONE-NIGHT STAND

I know you,
I know your love,
both timeless and pure.
Transcending, triumphant!
I can feel it,
tasting but never touched.

This girl I'm with isn't you,
isn't love.
What was I thinking?
I met her tonight
hoping it was you.
Another rushed failure,
but I'm so goddamn lonely!

I roll over,
away from this girl,
this body that promised pleasure,
yet brought only pain.
I stare out the window and wish
to forget this night,
to forget all of them.

PURE LOVE

When I'm alone,
I can be with you
   without hurting,
   without dying inside.
Pretend love is pure love—
   the purest I'll ever know.

My Life is Slow Death

Of all the emotions,
I feel Pain more than others.
It hits harder, cuts deeper,
    under the skin.
I am built for Pain, born to suffer!
My life is slow death
with joys that are few and fleeting.
That is why I must take care
to protect myself
and limit my exposure to Pain.
    I have enough of my own,
        I cannot take yours as well.

BETTER THIS WAY

Behind my eyes,
an unbreakable tomb:
    buried secrets,
    hidden doubt,
    sealed against future hurt.
The walls so thick,
you can't get in,
I can't get out.

    It's better this way.

Five Words

"Nobody loves me, nobody cares."

I'm pacing now,
repeating it like a mantra,
like the curse it is.

    Five words that define me,
    five words that destroy me,
    and I say them just for you.

ABANDONED, BETRAYED

The day I needed you most
   was the day
      you weren't there at all.

Waiting to Die

I live like I'm homeless:
    clothes ripped-up,
    trash everywhere.
I have money,
but don't deserve nice things.
The depression's so loud,
I can't hear myself think . . .

It takes all I have to write this.
I don't expect you to understand.
How can you, when even I don't understand
why I am the way I am?

Riders on the Bus

We're riders on the bus,
thinking we're going somewhere
when we're going nowhere at all.
We drive around in circles,
hoping salvation is only one stop away.

See the ugly woman yell at her ugly child:
    The little boy knows he's bad
    because his mother tells him so,
    and he will grow up to be bad.
    The jails are full of bad little boys
    in the bodies of men.
    They are there because their mothers
    didn't love them,
    didn't teach them to love themselves
    and so they expect the world to love them,
    but we all know what a heartache that is.

Now see the skinny man with nervous eyes:
    He travels alone except for the voices in his head,
    the voices that tell him he's no good,
    no good at all,
    and that if he could just find
    the right combination of drugs
    maybe the voices would be quiet.
    But there is no right combination,

there is only the promise put forth in cheap alleys
and expensive hospitals.
So the skinny man carries a hammer,
waiting for the voices to tell him what to do.
Maybe it will be his skull he cracks open,
or maybe it will be yours.
Either way, it's a relief.

And in the back of the bus,
see the homeless bums and lazy youth:
    fighting, laughing,
    going crazy with the knowledge
    that this is all there is,
    all there will ever be.
    See them, judge them,
    but we're no better
    because we're here too.

We're all riders on the bus.
We buy our ticket to this life
the same way we buy our death:
    one day at a time.

GRAY

I'm barely forty and my beard is gray.
My balls are gray,
    and this heavy feeling I carry inside,
    that's gray too.
I look outside my window—
    the world is gray.
The city and the street are dull with it.
I watch all the other gray people
    going to work or to church.
I see them going to buy
    bland food,
    bland clothes,
    bland books.
I see them coming home,
    their skin even grayer than before,
    with little pink children in tow.
I watch the children and smile,
knowing they'll be gray soon enough.

Alphabet of Suffering

Abandoned by everyone.
Betrayed by your friends.
Cynical of others.
Despised by society.
Exhausted from the struggle.
Frightened to go on.
Guilty of crimes real and imagined.
Humiliated in public.
Ill in your mind.
Jaded til nothing gives pleasure.
Kicked like a dog.
Lost in the crowd.
Misunderstanding the truth.
Nervously reaching out.
Overreacting to everything.
Pain all the time.
Quivering in fear.
Repulsed by your body.
Screaming for help.
Traumatized by family.
Undone by trusting the wrong people.
Victimized til you bleed.
Wounded in your soul.
Xenophobic of strangers.
Yelling in anger until you become a
Zealot, your life lost to an unworthy cause.

Family

I died the day I was born,
the day you came into my life.
Wanted, but never understood.
Rejected.
Clinging to hope—
    mad hope, mad fear.
Dying to get out.
I lived for your love,
yet never found it.

HELL IS MY HOME ADDRESS

I grew up in Hell,
    and not finding love,
        sought the hatred of others.

Another Holiday in Hell

Through the awkward silence,
I stare across the table at my family:
    Welcome to another holiday in hell.
We feast on hate and regret,
    drinking the wine of sorrow.
Why do we do it?
Why do we sit here and pretend,
    when deep down, we know
    we are too broken to go on?

The Happiest Time of the Year

Christmas is a shit season,
    a season for guilt and greed,
        for getting drunk and beating people up—
            yourself, mostly.
It is a time to reflect on a life un-lived,
    a dream denied.
It is snowstorms and rain
    crushed by gray, gray skies.
There is no sun anymore,
    there is only the cold, dismal and wet.
You can feel it in your bones.
They ache as you shiver.
There is a cough in your throat
    and snot in your nose.
You think of summer, how nice it will be,
    and all the things that you'll do . . .
        but you won't.
These are the fantasies you tell yourself every year,
    like how you'll get a new car or a new house,
    maybe a new lover—
        the old one's all used up, not that you can do better.
So you drink your whiskey and pop your pills
    as the fireplace roars,
        burning the night to embers and your soul to ash.
You sit there in the dark, slowly going mad
    pretending it's the happiest time of the year.

Government Cheesecake

I get on the bus and pay my last dollar
to get to the food bank.
Standing in line,
I hate the smell of my neighbors.
They stink of unwashed souls and dirty minds.
Small minds, always judging.
    But I'll fool them!
I can get unlimited bread and rice,
but only one dessert.
I hope they have cheesecake.
The voices in my head like cheesecake
almost as much as murder.

BROKEN DREAMS

Your broken dreams fall on my heart
   like meaningless autumn leaves.
      I light a match and watch them burn.

Garbage People

Garbage people with garbage brains,
grasping hands wanting more,
giving less.
They beg for help,
yet offer nothing in return.

A Warning to Girls

There are no magic rainbows
that can brighten your future.
All the mermaids and unicorns
can't save you from this
pink neon hell called Life
or the men who call it home.

America

I saw a car burning by the side of the road.
I didn't get out to help,
but I did slow down to watch.

It's All the Same

The man in rags rages
while the man in silk despairs.
Both are sick of themselves
and this world they've made—
    this planet called Hell.

DRIFTING

There are no enlightened rulers,
no enlightened masses.
There is only you, only me:
    lost,
        drifting on a burning sea of madness.

Right and Wrong

When the wrong man is right,
    no one listens.
When the right man is wrong,
    nations bleed.

It's Killing Us

It's war all the time, as Bukowski said:
    War on this, war on that.
Borders are drawn, lives lost,
and for what?
What does it matter when
it's not about who's right,
but who wins?

Meanwhile, the politicians lie,
the corporations sell,
the church converts people into profits
and prophets into people.
It used to be the only sure things were death and taxes,
but now you can count on:
    no privacy,
    no freedom,
    nobody and nothing
    except greed—the almighty dollar.
The American Way is killing us,
and we're not the only ones doing it,
but we're supposed to be better than that . . .
    or was that a lie too?

Circling the Drain

As rabid dogs howl and garbagemen close in,
as women weep and children scream,
packs of devils swoop overhead
to the sound of air raid sirens.
This then, is the end—
    the end of you and me, this whole stinking world
    awash with beer-flecked lips and stinking sheets.
Behold, the misery made from millions
who mistook sex for love, and love for sex.
The fragrant whores paint their lips with lies,
their bellies swollen, filled with rotten fruit.
Another poor bastard is born
    into this hell of blood and piss,
    the doctor hitting him on the ass—
    not to make him breathe,
    but to hear him scream.
    "Get used to it," the doctor says.
    "There's plenty more where that came from!"
And overhead, the devils laugh,
    grinning like vultures
    circling the drain
    of your life.

Weakness

For a man, weakness is hard to show
and harder to share,
but for a woman, it is everything.

SELF-DECEPTION

What is right is never easy,
but what is wrong—
    we all do a little of that everyday.
And if we do the wrong thing too well,
    or too often,
it begins to look right.
    That's when we're fucked
    when we could have been saved.

The Gondola of My Fears

The gondola of my fears glides deeper
into the city of my mind.
Memories rise like water,
reminding me of times
best left submerged
and forgotten . . .

Civil War

When you're at war with yourself,
   everyone begins to look like
      an enemy.

REGRET

You are the weed in the garden of my mind.
   I pull you up, only to unearth more pain:
      The sorrow of the life un-lived,
         the path not taken.
            Why are there so many of you?

— Part Three —
THE GHOST IN ME
(Meditations on Life, Death, and Beyond)

The Long, Slow Monday

This is the long, slow Monday.
The birth of many spent sitting,
waiting to be set free—
    not of this thankless job,
    but from this boring world.

    Tell me:
        How many Mondays til then?

These Shoes, They Travel

These shoes, they travel
through stunted streets and shadowed woods,
but I have no idea where they're going.
My soul left my body a long time ago.
Only this flesh remains,
this fractured mind
going through the motions of life
enjoying none of it.

THE BITTER DAYS OF AUTUMN

The bitter days of autumn burst red,
falling leaves that carry
   empty hopes,
   wasted years.
I can smell them all
rotting in the forest of my mind.

Without Hope

Your lies left me bleeding on a sea of regret.
The sharks circle in, closer now.
I am too hurt to fight, too spent to care.
   Just one bite,
    and I'm gone . . .

The Worst Way to Die

At sea, there are three ways to die:
    the propeller, the shark, or to drown.

On land, there are many more ways,
    but the worst one, the deadliest,
        is loneliness.

Loneliness kills slower and is more cruel
than all the guns, all the knives,
and every disease.
Each year, it gets harder to avoid:
    friends and family die, get married,
        or run away.
Children and pets do the same.
Even your wife has to go some day.
What will you do then?
How will you fight the soul-crushing isolation?
The day-to-day horror of an empty house?

On land, everyone leaves sooner or later.
The sea is simpler, cleaner.
There is no loneliness here,
    only the velvet deep
        welcoming you home . . .

Worthless

Last night I told my cat
I was going to kill her.
She kept trying
to climb my bookshelf,
claws sinking into spines,
shredding pages.
I'd been trying to sleep
    (not very successfully),
and her bullshit wasn't helping.
I growled and hissed,
squirting her with water,
chasing her around the house screaming,
    "I'll kill you! You used to be good,
    but now you're worthless.
    Nobody loves you.
    No one will miss you when you're gone!"
The cat stared at me
with big, scared eyes.
I realized then
I wasn't talking to her at all:

I was talking to myself.

The Mystery Tree

The old, gnarled oak stood tall in my youth:
    proud, unyielding.
The Druids would have fallen to their knees to worship it,
    that's how beautiful it was.
We called it "The Mystery Tree,"
and it was where we held our Monster Club meetings.
We were a group of first-graders
high on PopTarts and Scooby-Doo.
We knew the woods were full of monsters,
but our parents said they were only bums.
hard men fallen on hard times.
    But to us, they were mystical warlocks,
    hermits possessed of secret knowledge.
    They knew what magic lurked in those woods
    but never told us.
They never got the chance:
    Tom fell out of the Mystery Tree and broke his arm,
    Bobby got chased by a hobo.
After that, our parents wouldn't let us play in the woods.
The Monster Club disbanded,
friendships faded:
    lost to time,
    to girls,
    to anything but the pursuit of magic
    and true adventure.
But I never forgot the Mystery Tree:

the power it held in its crooked branches,
the power to capture our imagination.
It was special—sacred and sublime.
I'd spent hours there, learning how to climb,
and when I got as high as I could get,
I'd snuggle against the trunk
and put my brain to work
dreaming of the man I would become . . .
>   *Rich, famous, loved.*
>   *Everything I ever saw on TV and more.*

Years went by, some of them good,
>   most of them not,
>   and a few that were awful beyond words.
I got to thinking about the Mystery Tree,
how it was the one thing I could always count on—
>   not family, not friends,
>   just this goddamn, beautiful tree.
I had to see it again,
so I made the trip home through rain and snow.
I was at a crossroads in my life.
I needed that tree more than ever,
and not just the tree, but what it represented.
If I could just touch its bark,
take shelter in its branches,
inspiration would strike
and a new dream would come . . .

Only when I got there, the Mystery Tree was gone

along with the woods.
The faceless bastards who ruin everything
had paved it over with an office park,
like they paved over my life.
I was crying when I got back into my car,
crying for the first time in years,
and I couldn't stop.

I drove into the hills, away from the cruel city,
into the dark, silent woods.
There were no lights there, no people,
just me and the Mystery Tree's brothers.
I laughed and cried and laughed some more,
then I screamed.

The Doors came on the radio,
urging me to "Break On Through."
I pointed my car toward the nearest cliff
and crashed through the guard rail.

On the way down, I said goodbye
to all the wild places of this world,
to all the mysteries,
all the magic,
and the little boy who dared to believe.

END OF THE LINE

I walk this lonely road,
ripped-up and ragged.
    Thumb out,
    hopes down.
Waiting for a ride,
waiting for someone
    to pick me up
and finally give a damn,
but no one does.

The sun sets, the hours fade.
I lie down in the road
    tired, undone.
If you will not stop for me,
then I must stop for you.

Might as Well Enjoy It

If you're going to hang yourself,
   do it right!
With your pants around your ankles,
   rubbing one out,
   fucking life
   the way life fucked you.
Rent a tux with a red carnation.
Get your hair cut and your shoes shined.
Leave a beautiful corpse,
   the kind to make your landlady blush.

SUICIDE SOLUTION

One bullet is all I need
   to make me forget you
      the way you forgot me.

SUICIDE NOTE

In a tub full of anger, I bleed.
It didn't have to end this way:
    razored wrists,
        empty heart.
Yours is the last name I speak.

Meat Suit

What is this frail body?
This cursed flesh?
    A prison cage
    enslaving me to animal needs,
    animal hungers!
My soul tires of this wretched frame,
worn down by the apathy of others,
the tireless cruelty of self.
    I could end this life,
    but what would replace it?

Some new body in a far worse place?
    Some ghostly torment?
        Or nothing at all?

A Meditation on Death

In winter, you can see your breath,
but not your soul.

You must be colder for that.

This Dusty Soul

While Japanese girls giggle behind their hands,
while the books I bought go unread
and my favorite TV shows record,
I grow another year older:
    wrinkles on my face,
    cobwebs in my mind.
This dusty soul shrugs but does not laugh.
I thought I'd have more time:
    time to find you,
    time to find myself,
    to amount to something.
Instead, I have a house full of stuff I don't need
and no one I do.

Nursing Home Blues

I am old and ugly.
Unloved, unwanted,
I walk this path alone,
popping pills, wasting time.
How much longer have I got?
    My dentures don't fit,
    my ass hurts,
    my bones ache,
    and I've got a bedsore on my soul.
I try to tell the nurse,
but no one listens anymore.

Time is a Bastard

I am an old man dribbling piss
down the leg of the world.
Mouthing silent curses,
shaking my cane
at a planet gone mad,
a nation in ruins.
    Hating myself,
      the slow march of time,
      the passing of days
      like the crawling of insects.
I was someone once, I mattered!
I was going to do big things,
perform miracles.
But Time is a bastard.
It keeps slipping away,
sneaking off like a thief,
like a lover who has tired of me.

    What is left for me now
        but to die alone?

Done

In the end, after all the struggling,
and all the protests,
we want the same thing:
    to let this life end
    quickly, easily,
    without pain or senility.
It doesn't matter if we go to heaven or hell,
if we reincarnate, or remain as ghosts.
    Our bodies are done.

The Disappointed Life

I have no hope for anyone,
least of all myself.
The days pass, colorless gray.
All my life, I have been waiting to die.

Now, as the hour approaches,
I suspect even death must disappoint . . .

This Amnesiac World

It is only by the luxury of death
I have the time for clarity,
even a little wisdom.
Too late, of course,
to change anything,
to make this broken body
and brittle mind
rise from my grave.
No, it's too late for me,
but I can tell you one thing:

There's a storm coming.
A storm that will wash you away
And everything you've done.

This amnesiac world
will go on without you,
as if you never were.
Fighting the same fights,
hating the same hates.
Fearing, destroying,
until the last of us is dead.

LIKE FLOWERS

The gutter is my grave.
    This building, my tombstone.
      The people walk by,
          the treading of their feet
        like flowers.

The Show Must Go On

How many days have we felt
desperate to make the pain stop,
the world end?
But no matter how loud we scream,
   no one hears,
   no one cares.
The show must go on . . .

When No One Cares

Sometimes,
I think the whole world's insane.
Other times,
I think I'm crazy to love,
crazy to hate,
crazy to do nothing at all:
    stay,
    go,
    live,
    die.
What does it matter
when no one cares?

THE STRUGGLE

In this desperate dying,
    the struggle is not for others
        to find meaning in me,
            but for me to find meaning
                in myself.

The Problem with Words

Lies are easy.
The truth is hard:
    hard to comprehend,
    hard to speak.
It slips through your fingers like sand.

BLIND

Most people are too blind to see
    there is always a way
        out of the Dark.

SOMETHING FOR NOTHING

When all you have is Nothing,
it becomes Something:
    either what drives you
        or what destroys you.

And Soon, the Snow

Midnight in December:
    The whole world lies still, waiting,
    except for me.
I have to get out, have to think.
Hands in pockets, I walk on,
away from you and your poisonous doubt.
My breath mists,
frozen leaves crunch underfoot.
    It will snow soon,
    but not enough to bury me
    or my dreams.

Everyday, There Are People

Everyday, there are people:
    People who live,
    people who die.
Which kind will you be?

If You Want My Advice

Start living.
    You'll be dead
        soon enough.

The Strangest Places

When you don't know where you're going,
you arrive in the strangest places:
    ghost towns and graveyards,
    train tracks to nowhere.
Each has a story to tell
if you only stop to listen.
But the sky is dark and the rain comes down.
You drive on, oblivious to how close you came
to meeting those ghosts,
to hearing their tales of a life and death
not unlike your own.

The Road Within

Before I found myself I found you:
    The Open Road.
Whenever life got me down,
I would climb behind the wheel and drive
trying to get lost on purpose.
It was an adventure.
I kept hoping I'd find a secret portal,
a rift between worlds,
one that would take me far away
to some bright and shining land,
a place where I could be a hero,
a place where people would love me . . .
I never found that place in my car.
I had to find it in myself,
and in these words I write to you.

Nobody's Perfect

You will be mocked
    for being you who are,
    looking like you do.
For not being the kind of perfect
    you see in magazines, in movies or TV.
But the truth is
    those "perfect" people are anything but.
They're just like us,
    only they have money for:
        plastic surgery,
        personal trainers,
        Photoshop experts,
        stylists,
        and fancy clothes.
But that's all they have.
These are things anyone with
    the right money and connections can enjoy,
    but money doesn't make you special,
    it just makes you rich.
It's all an illusion,
    a sad, plastic dream.
So do what you can with your outside
    (if you must),
    but don't lose any sleep over it,
    and don't spend years starving yourself
    or beating yourself up in the mirror.

Work on your inner beauty instead,
    that quality we all possess.
The sooner you look for it,
    the sooner you'll find it,
        and the happier you'll be.

At Peace, At Last

I embrace the damaged parts of me:
    I love them,
    forgive them,
    and understand their pain.
I rock them to sleep
and heal them,
finding myself
at peace, at last.

No Looking Back

There is no looking back.
There is only the path we are on,
this constant motion carrying us
from our awful past
    into
a brilliant future.

Ready for the Rain

I'm ready for the rain
to come and wash away
 this lie,
 this name,
 this past,
all these broken, crippled things.
Pain I've asked for,
pain I've given,
a hundred dying fears
that will not go quietly but must.

I'm ready for the rain
to make me new again.

You Know You're Getting Old

You know you're getting old
when you can't stand
    the music,
    the fashion,
    the slang,
    the sound of young voices laughing.
You know you're getting old when you crave
    peace,
    quiet,
    security,
    a warm bed and soft lap to call home.
And that's all right,
    that's how it should be . . .
The pain and confusion go away,
    replaced by wisdom and a kind of sadness,
    a resignation that no,
    you didn't change the world.
You never had a chance,
    but you did the best you could
    with what you had.
And in the end, it was enough.

OLD SOULS

Old souls often die young,
compressing an entire life
into a few decades,
knowing what to say
in the fewest words,
knowing what to do
in the fewest actions—

Like this.

Always a Challenge

The name you were born with
   is not who you are.
Neither is your face,
   your body,
   or anything you do.
Who you are is
   a bright and shining soul
      locked in a dark and desperate world.
Trapped in this flesh,
   this form,
   this lie.
You can see it
   as punishment,
   a test, or a game,
   but is always a challenge.
It never stops.
Our bodies do, but our souls don't.
They start over
   in new bodies
   with new names and new lives,
   hoping this time will be
      the last time,
      the best time,
   the time we finally unlock the door
   to end this earthly cycle
      and begin the next.

BUKOWSKI'S GHOST

I am a god among poets,
and a poet among gods.
I walk the road between
reality and dreams
shedding lies,
spreading truths,
and all things in-between.

The Ghost in Me

Shall I tell you the story of how I came to be?
I was a soul, floating alone
when I came into a body that didn't want to live.
    I became that body.
    It was not the best body.
    It was not the most handsome or strong,
    but it had a keen mind, and it would do.
There was much confusion and pain
integrating myself while disintegrating the old—
    vestiges of its past life, decades of pain.
The body had few family or friends,
but I did not come here to socialize,
    I came to create!
    And so I shall.
Despite the pain, despite the hardships,
I foresee great things:
    visions of my words changing lives,
    moving people . . .
Toward what, I don't know,
but the fact that I make them
feel and move at all
seems enough for now.

My Poetry Manifesto

ADVICE TO NEW POETS

To write good poetry, abandon everything you've been taught. Good poetry rarely rhymes or uses flowery, stilted language. It is not bound by strict rules, but by emotion. Good poetry comes from the heart, from hope, from pain. Good poetry is not obscure in its meaning. It is simple and direct, the language of the soul. A poem that cannot do this is a poem best left forgotten.

For your first poem, don't overdo it. Start small. Three-lines is easier than five, and five is easier than ten. Go slow, there's no rush. Eventually, you'll be able to pull off a full-page or more.

The best poems come easily, like opening a vein. The worst are the ones you have to force. Don't be afraid to abandon the ones that aren't working, or come back to them later when you find fresh inspiration.

As for content, write about what matters to you: *your pain, your love*. Share yourself. Be shameless. Be fearless. But above all, be yourself.

— JDC

We need magic to give our existence meaning.

Poems to Ignite and Inspire — Coming Soon!

ABOUT THE AUTHOR

Jackson Dean Chase brings you Bold Visions of Dark Places. He is the #1 bestselling author of over a dozen Young Adult titles and nonfiction books for writers. His adult poetry includes *Bukowski's Ghost (Poems for Old Souls in New Bodies)* and *Love at the Bottom of the Litter Box (Bukowski, Cats, and Me)*.

Thank you for buying *Bukowski's Ghost!*

If you enjoyed this book, please leave an online review. Even if it's just a few lines, your words can make a difference to help reach new readers.

Have a question or suggestion? Or just want to say hi?

Jackson loves to connect with his fans! Friend or follow him online.

- **Website:** JacksonDeanChase.com
- **Facebook:** facebook.com/jacksondeanchase
- **Tumblr:** JacksonDeanChase.tumblr.com
- **Twitter:** @Jackson_D_Chase
- **Email:** jackson@jacksondeanchase.com

Want to know when Jackson's next book is coming out?

Sign up and get **FREE BOOKS** at: www.JacksonDeanChase.com
There's NO SPAM, and your email address will never be shared.

With *Love at the Bottom of the Litter Box*, Jackson Dean Chase delivers a stunning poetry chapbook that delivers the sweet pain and subtle humor of life on the edge. **Experience it!**

eBook and Trade Paperback available now

Love at the Bottom of the Litter Box collects every poem by Jackson Dean Chase that mentions cats, including these soulful gems:

You Had Me at "Meow"

You had me at "meow," my friend.
You had me with three sleepy blinks,
with the tender flick of your tail,
the purr in your throat.
You had me with all these things:
treasured moments
curling in my lap.

Today

Today is the day when love lies dreaming
    as Mexicans cut my grass,
    as cats yowl and dogs bark,
    as the phone rings and bills mount,
    as my parents inch toward their graves,
    and I speed toward mine,
    somewhere, a girl thinks of me
    and I, of her.
We shared something once,
a moment of passion.
Now we share this memory
and wonder what might have been . . .

Nuke Writer's Block Forever!

Writing so hot, it's radioactive! Come along for the ride as #1 bestselling author Jackson Dean Chase takes you deep into the twisted ruins of a new tomorrow. If you write Apocalyptic, Post-Apocalyptic, Dystopian, Prepper, or Zombie fiction, don't to be caught without this!

eBook and Trade Paperback available now

This Time, It's Personal...

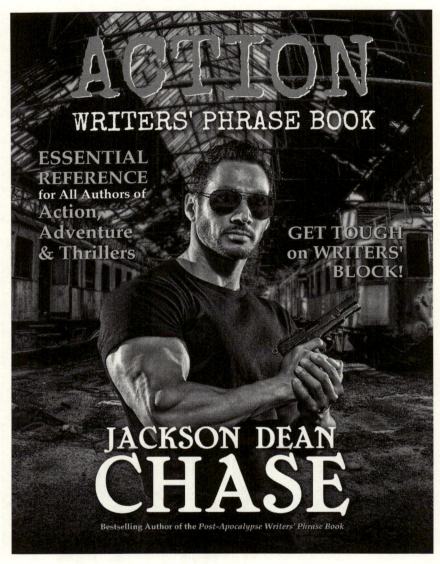

Hey, you! Tired of your imagination hitting a brick wall? Pump up your mental muscles with the *Action Writers' Phrase Book*. With over 2,000 ways to describe weapons, fights, and more, it's the perfect workout for authors of Action, Adventure, and Thrillers!

eBook and Trade Paperback available now

GET READY FOR GHASTLY TERROR!

The most shocking Young Adult Horror stories ever written!
Zombies, Maniacs, and more are waiting to rip your mind apart in this spellbinding collection from #1 bestselling author Jackson Dean Chase. ***Warning:*** *These stories may be too extreme for some readers!*

eBook and Trade Paperback available now

BEWARE THE LOVE OF THE DAMNED!

Finally, YA Horror with bite! A lonely teen sells her soul to become a vampire, only to discover that becoming a monster will forever deny her the love she craves. This is a chilling, realistic journey into what it would *really* be like to become a vampire . . .

eBook and Trade Paperback coming soon

Made in the USA
Middletown, DE
25 August 2018